TWELVE DAYS OF

Silent
Nights

From the author of *A Daily Catholic Moment* and *My Year with the Saints for Kids* comes a book about the most popular Christmas song in the world, the Nativity of Jesus Christ, and how to carry the beauty and wonder of the Bethlehem stable into our lives as a new year begins. Celano reflects on "Silent Night, Holy Night"—how it came to be, its continued importance, and its message of contemplation, hope, and love. The year 2019 marks the 200th anniversary of the first major performances of the carol.

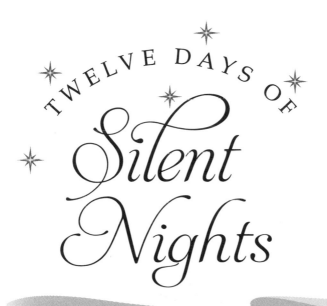

TWELVE DAYS OF

Silent Nights

THE STORY BEHIND THE MOST POPULAR
CHRISTMAS CAROL, THE BIRTH OF CHRIST,
AND WHAT IT MEANS FOR OUR LIVES

PETER CELANO

PARACLETE PRESS

Brewster, Massachusetts

2019 First Printing

Twelve Days of Silent Nights: The Story Behind the Most Popular Christmas Carol, and How to Apply Its Timeless Wisdom to Our Lives

Copyright © 2019 Paraclete Press, Inc.

ISBN 978-1-64060-337-0

The Paraclete Press name and logo (dove on cross) are trademarks of Paraclete Press, Inc.

Library of Congress Cataloging-in-Publication Data

Names: Celano, Peter, author.
Title: Twelve days of silent nights : the story behind the most popular Christmas carol, the birth of Christ, and what it means for our lives / Peter Celano.
Description: Brewster, Massachusetts : Paraclete Press, 2019.
Identifiers: LCCN 2019011812 | ISBN 9781640603370 (hard cover, self cover)
Subjects: LCSH: Gruber, Franz Xaver, 1787-1863. Stille Nacht, heilige Nacht. | Mohr, Joseph, 1792-1848. Stille Nacht, heilige Nacht. | Christmas.
Classification: LCC ML410.G94 C45 2019 | DDC 782.28/1723--dc23
LC record available at https://lccn.loc.gov/2019011812

10 9 8 7 6 5 4 3 2 1

Published by Paraclete Press
Brewster, Massachusetts
www.paracletepress.com
Printed in the United States of America

THIS BOOK IS DEDICATED TO
carolers and choirs everywhere.
Keep singing!

CONTENTS

✴ 4 ✴

Our Silent Nights,
from
CHRISTMAS DAY TO JANUARY 5
49

✴ ✴ ✴

TWELVE DAYS OF

Silent
Nights

1

Christmas Eve

1818
NORTH OF SALZBURG

I magine a snowy evening in one of the old small towns of Austria, eleven miles north of Salzburg—in a little village called Oberndorf. The year is 1818. A schoolmaster and a priest are quickly rehearsing for Midnight Mass.

Father Joseph Mohr was a young twenty-six. He had written a poem, "Stille Nacht," two years earlier. Schoolmaster Franz Xaver Gruber was thirty-one and was a teacher in the primary school in nearby Arnsdorf. Father Mohr had asked Schoolmaster Gruber if he thought his six-stanza poem might perhaps be suitable for song lyrics, and if so, could Gruber, an accomplished church musician, possibly try his hand at the music.

Innsbruck,
aquatint, ca. 1830

3

The little parish church where they were standing was named for *Sankt Nikolaus*, as St. Nicholas's name is rendered in German. This is the St. Nicholas who was an ancient Christian bishop from Greek Asia Minor, and who became known during his lifetime for leaving gifts for children, even dropping them down chimneys. He wouldn't become the ubiquitous St. Nick of Christmas festivities and lore until later. Just five years after Mohr talked to Gruber in 1823, a distinguished seminary professor in America, Clement Clarke Moore, would write what became another famous poem, "A Visit from St. Nicholas." If you're wondering, *Why don't I know this poem, if it is famous?*, it is because you know it by its other name: the poem was soon retitled "'Twas the Night Before Christmas"—for its first line.

The name of the church where the pastor and the schoolmaster were standing seems almost providential.

So, we return to December 24, 1818. Christmas Eve that year is where the story of "Silent Night, Holy Night" begins. There, in St. Nikolaus Church, Mohr and Gruber huddled, energetically rehearsing the music Gruber had written earlier that day to go with the lyrics of his friend. It was dark outside. People were making their way to Mass. The priest and the schoolmaster stood alone in the quiet church, which was lighted only by candles.

Long before we became accustomed to priestly musicians, Father Mohr played the guitar that night, as the two men performed the carol to a delighted congregation. Both this music and these words were special. As the people were arriving for Mass, Father Mohr was plucking out the chords, first finding his way through the simple, beautiful tune.

The famous Christmas carol "Silent Night, Holy Night" is a product of two inspired Austrian men of faith. Even so, a century later, it was the subject of misuse during the First World War in Germany, when the original lyrics were rewritten to support a war. Germans were told by their Kaiser to sing the new version; but with the original tune unchanged, many knew that the spirit had been corrupted. This was a tragic instance of intention to destroy what had become almost gospel. How could Christians abandon a wish and a prayer for peace for people everywhere? Something similar took place once again, during the Nazi reign in Germany another twenty or so years later, when Adolf Hitler sought to be praised as a savior, and "Silent Night" was rewritten once more. Again, we can assume, Christians knew the difference.

If you ever have an opportunity to visit Salzburg, Austria, today, you might want to see the birthplace of Wolfgang Amadeus Mozart and the setting of the great twentieth-century musical *The Sound of Music*. But be sure, too, to visit the *Stille-Nacht-Kapelle*, or Silent Night

Chapel, in nearby Oberndorf, and its adjacent museum. The original St. Nikolaus Church is no longer standing, having been long ago destroyed by a flood. But in the Silent Night Chapel in Oberndorf you can still see many artifacts relating to Fr. Mohr and Mr. Gruber. And if you happen to be there on Christmas Eve, you can attend a memorial Mass during which "Silent Night" is movingly sung in a variety of languages. The spirit—as it was intended—lives on.

Today, "Silent Night" is the most popular Christmas carol in the world. We know this by the number of copyrighted recordings that have been made of the song: more than twice as many as the second most popular Christmas carol, "Joy to the World."

The year after that first performance in the little St. Nikolaus Church in Oberndorf, news spread of the beauty of the composition and lyrics. An organist, who was either there that night or who heard one of the early performances, fell in love with the song and carried the composition back to his hometown, sharing it with others, there. Then, two traveling families of singers (*The Sound of Music* von Trapps of the early twentieth century in Salzburg were examples of such singing families, who have a long and venerable history in Austria!) caught on to the song, and they began adding "Silent Night" to their regular repertoire the following year, 1819. Just

Reproduction of the actual page for "Silent Night! Holy Night"
from John Freeman Young's *Carols for Christmas Tide*, 1859.

one generation later, "Silent Night" was even being requested by the king himself, Frederick William IV of Prussia.

"Silent Night" made its way to America at about the same time that the king of Prussia was requesting it at his court during Christmastide. The venue for the carol in the United States couldn't have been more prestigious. It was the Reverend John Freeman Young, of Trinity Church on Wall Street in New York City, who took up the translation of "Stille Nacht, Heilige Nacht" into English. Trinity Church, in lower Manhattan, is a historic parish church, perhaps the most historic in the still-young American colonies, famous for its influential location on Wall Street as well as for the immensity of its financial endowment. Both location and revenue for the church can be traced back to the late seventeenth century, nearly a century before the United States of

America separated from the British Empire, when Trinity received its original charter and land from King William III of England. That land, which was then full of cows, quickly became lower Manhattan!

While an assistant minister at Trinity Church, Reverend Young published a booklet titled *Carols for Christmas Tide*, in 1859, and it included his original English translation of the great German-language carol. The booklet was used in all the religious services at Trinity Church that year, and "Silent Night, Holy Night" caught on quickly.

Only the first three stanzas were included. This is the carol as millions of English-speaking people have sung it ever since that time.

After that first Christmas in America, Young's booklet was often copied, and his translation of "Silent Night," as well as the musical setting of the song, was greatly admired by people of all denominational backgrounds. It was a combination of Young's excellent work, and the position of influence of Trinity Church, that then spread the Austrian carol all over the United States and beyond, throughout the English-speaking world.

Despite the rapid spread of the carol, and its translation into dozens of languages, it would be another fifty years before it was recorded by a world-renowned group, the Haydn Quartet. Two tenors, one bass, and one baritone, they titled their release "Silent Night, Hallowed Night," and that's how they rendered the opening line, changing slightly the translation of Rev. Young of Trinity Church. (As anyone knows who is familiar with singing "Silent Night," the word "holy" is intoned slowly over three syllables; "hall-ow-ed" actually fits the music better.) The Haydn Quartet recording was released on the Victor label, and described as a Christmas hymn (Victor matrix

B-2784). Their recording of two minutes and eight seconds from 1905 is still available today. In fact, we've preserved a copy on our website. You can listen to it by typing this link into your browser:

https://www.youtube.com/watch?v=E_DeUsVcQoY

2
"Silent Night" and
THE NATIVITY

ilent Night, Holy Night" has become an essential part of our celebration of the Nativity—Christmas Day.

Christmas is preceded by the season of Advent. It is Advent that initiates the season of Christmastide—a liturgical term that means, simply, Christmastime, or the Christmas season. In most churches, Christmas or Christmastide begins in the evening on Christmas Eve. It is at that evening service, or at home, as we celebrate the arrival in Bethlehem of Mary and Joseph, who are preparing for the birth of Christ, that we mark the border between Advent's conclusion and the beginning of the celebration of Christmas.

The Nativity,
vintage engraving.

Why do these distinctions and definitions matter? Each season, each day, is meant to carry us through our faith—guiding us in recalling and understanding the life of Christ. Advent prepares us for the coming of Christ (both the coming that took place in Bethlehem, and the second coming, which we await in the future). But at Christmas Eve, the tone changes. This is why this great Christmas hymn is so perfect for that night, which is more special than any other night. It marks the most pivotal moment in world history.

When we sing "Silent Night" today, we usually sing at most three stanzas, corresponding to what were Fr. Mohr's original composition's first, sixth, and second verses of the carol. What follows are reflections on all six of the original stanzas, beginning with those familiar three, then including translations of the three much-lesser-known verses.

STANZA 1

There are some almost universal effects that "Silent Night, Holy Night" has upon us when we sing it. "Silent Night" quiets us. It makes us sit still. We are hushed—quite willingly, as we sing—by the solemn imagining of an occasion that is described at first as simply "silent" and "holy." The words of the carol, and its hushed tone (you cannot—you should not ever—sing this carol loudly), make us feel as if we are there at the Nativity, in that very stable where the Christ child first lay.

The Nativity itself quiets us in this way. It is at that moment, when Christ is born among us, that we find ourselves singing "Silent Night." We know that Christ is still among us. We see him in Mary's arms. Even animals that might otherwise be baying or crowing are silent in the presence of such simple holiness.

Silent night, holy night,

All is calm, all is bright

Round yon Virgin Mother and Child.

Holy Infant, so tender and mild,

Sleep in heavenly peace,

Sleep in heavenly peace.

STANZA 2

There were very few people nearby when Christ was born in those humble circumstances. The shepherds on the hills must have seen Joseph and Mary on the road, as they walked on their way. They might have seen them, too, knocking on the door of the inn where they were told there was no room. And they probably realized that the Holy Family then ended up settling among farm animals in the Bethlehem stable.

When the baby was born, they knew he was special. How did they know? Angels revealed to them the truth. As the Gospel of Luke relays, the scene happened at night:

In that region there were shepherds living in the fields, keeping watch over their flock by night. Then an angel of the Lord stood before them, and the glory of the Lord shone around them, and they were terrified. But the angel said to them, "Do not be afraid; for see—I am bringing you good news of great joy for all the people: to you is born this day in the city of David a Savior, who is the Messiah, the Lord. This will be a sign for you: you will find a child wrapped in bands of cloth and lying in a manger." (Luke 2:8–12)

So, they came to see this child. And they adored him.

We adore him, today, when we sing "Silent Night." Part of what's special about "Silent Night" is the way the music reveals and relays a spirit of adoration; the music "puts" us in that spirit. We don't adore Christ by an act of will; our hearts have been taught the chords of the sweet music of adoration.

Silent night, holy night,
Shepherds quake at the sight;
Glories stream from heaven afar,
Heavenly hosts sing Alleluia!
Christ the Savior is born,
Christ the Savior is born!

STANZA 3

At the exact moment when the angel of the Lord told the shepherds in the hills that they had among them, "a Savior, who is the Messiah, the Lord," and pointed them to the manger in the nearby inn, where they might adore the Child, the text in Luke's Gospel goes on to immediately add: there was singing!

Who was singing?

And suddenly there was with the angel a multitude of the heavenly host, praising God and saying,
"Glory to God in the highest heaven,
and on earth peace among those whom he favors!" (Luke 2:13–14)

Angels—a "heavenly host." Those shepherds couldn't possibly have comprehended all that was meant by the advent of that simple, holy child in that homely bed. When we sing stanza three of "Silent Night," we, however, *do* comprehend. We might not have personal messages from angels (as those shepherds did!), but we have the benefit of the New Testament Gospels. As we sing, we are able to contemplate the longer view of salvation history that was first hinted by the angel of the Lord on the hillside that night in Bethlehem.

Silent night, holy night,
Son of God, love's pure light;
Radiant beams from Thy Holy Face
With the dawn of redeeming grace,
Jesus, Lord, at Thy birth,
Jesus, Lord, at Thy birth.

Nativity,
Martin Schongauer, engraving, ca.1435–1491

STANZA 4

These next three stanzas of "Silent Night" are virtually unknown to Christians today. They have only rarely been sung—either in German, or in English—since they were first written. Our translations are derived from others one can find, with some digging, but with slight changes for a more sonorous, poetic effect.

This stanza reminds us of what is central to our faith: God's grace toward us. The *Catechism of the Catholic Church* defines grace as "favor, the free and undeserved help that God gives us to respond to his call to become children of God, adoptive sons, partakers of the divine nature and of eternal life." Christians have argued about the means of grace, how much grace works in one's life apart from human act and decision, but all Christians agree that God's grace was made most evident in the advent of the Christ child for our salvation. So, we sing, with praise, "Here at last, healing light."

Silent night, holy night

Here at last, healing light

From the heavenly kingdom sent,

Grace abundant for our intent.

Jesus, salvation for all.

Jesus, salvation for all.

Mother and Child,
Albrecht Dürer, woodcut, 1519–1520

STANZA 5

There is a peace that comes from a relationship with God through Christ. That, too, is what we sing when we sing "Silent Night." We don't simply look upon the child with wonder and praise; we know what the child promises for us.

The world can be a frightening, disquieting place. Our lives are filled with what worries and disturbs us. It is sometimes tough to separate ourselves from those things. "Silent Night" and the Christmas season are a help. And, in singing, we're reminded that the world can sleep in peace tonight, of all nights, because at least for this moment we are certain of the peace that comes from God's sending his Son to us.

St. Paul wrote: "Let the peace of Christ rule in your hearts" (Colossians 3:15).

Silent night, holy night

The world sleeps in peace tonight.

God sends his Son to earth below

A Child from whom all blessings flow.

Jesus embraces mankind.

Jesus embraces mankind.

STANZA 6

Hopefully, you have by now begun to see how rich it can be to sing all the stanzas of "Silent Night, Holy Night." One hope behind this little book is the reinvigoration of our Decembers and our Christmastides with these words, many of which have been lost for two hundred years.

This final stanza is a summary of all of those that have preceded it. It is, in many respects, the loveliest to sing, and the one that best summarizes the simple and profound theology of the carol. Consider this reflection from one of the Old Testament prophets, as you sing:

"The LORD is in his holy temple;
let all the earth keep silence before him!"
(Habakkuk 2:20).

Silent night, holy night

Mindful of our sore plight

Lord in Heav'n on high decreed

Earthly woes from which we'd be freed.

Jesus, God's promised peace.

Jesus, God's promised peace.

❊ 3 ❊
Christmas Eve

six centuries earlier (December 24, 1223),
IN UMBRIA, ITALY...

When St. Francis of Assisi Created
the First Live Nativity

There was a man named John of Greccio, of holy reputation, and even better life, whom St. Francis of Assisi loved with special affection because, even though he was a man of noble and honorable position in town, he had trampled on the nobility of the flesh in order to follow a greater nobility of spirit.

St. Francis sent for John fifteen days before the Nativity of the Lord, and said to

Saint Francis with the Christ Child,
Pietro Faccini, etching, 1562–1602

43

him, "So that we may celebrate the festival, hurry ahead and prepare in Greccio what I tell you.

"I would like to make a memorial of the child born in Bethlehem so that people may behold with their very eyes how he lay in a manger on the hay, with the ox, and the donkey close by."

So John went and hurried to do as the saint instructed.

When Christmas Eve came, people from all around were invited to see what had been re-enacted in Greccio. With happy hearts, they came with candles to illuminate the night, remembering that first night when a radiant star showed Mary and Joseph the way to

Bethlehem. Then St. Francis came, and finding everything prepared, rejoiced. The manger had been made ready. Even hay was laid inside. There was a newborn baby in the arms of a young woman, and beside her was a man dressed as Joseph, and domestic animals just as there might have been on that first night.

There, in Greccio, as at the first holy Nativity, simplicity was honored, poverty was exalted, and humility was commended. They made Greccio as if it were a new Bethlehem.

The night was lit up as the day with the candles. The people had come, and at the reenacted Mystery they were rejoicing. The woods rang with voices. Against the rocks echoed the jubilant throng. The people sang praises to the Lord all night long. St. Francis stood before the manger, overcome with tenderness, filled with joy.

A priest celebrated the solemnities of the Mass over the manger, and everyone present was consoled. With sonorous voices, they

chanted the holy Gospel. Then Francis preached to the people with encouraging words about the birth of the poor King and the little town of Bethlehem. It was said that when, that night, Francis would say the name "Christ Jesus," and then "child of Bethlehem," so full of love and affection was his voice that "Bethlehem" came out sounding like a sheep bleating.

The gifts of God were multiplied that night, and a vision of wondrous effect of the Nativity was seen by everyone present. Amen.

Alleluia!

[adapted from Thomas of Celano's First Life of St. Francis, book 1, ch. 30]

The Nativity,
vintage engraving

GLORIA IN EXCELSIS DEO

* 4 *
Our Silent Nights,
from
CHRISTMAS DAY TO JANUARY 5

he Twelve Days of Christmas" is another Christmas carol sung so frequently that we rarely pause to consider what it means. Why are there two turtle doves? Why *French* hens?

The song—in both words and music—is either English or French in origin. No one really knows for certain. As you easily notice in singing it, it is what's called a cumulative song: each stanza builds upon the last. But toward what? And why? Some folklorists say that those stanzas, which are often baffling to us today (do partridges sit in pear trees? and if so, why does that matter?), were coded with religious meanings that have since been lost to Christians.

The Nativity,
Gustave Doré, engraving, 1891

Could it be that the song—which was first published in England during the roughly 175-year period when Catholicism was criminalized in England—is a sort of catechism? We have seen, for instance, these explanations for meanings that might be coded in each of the twelve days of Christmas, according to the carol:

A partridge in a pear tree Jesus Christ

Two turtle doves The Old and New Testaments

Three French hens The three theological[1] virtues: faith, hope, and love

Four calling birds The four Gospels: Matthew, Mark, Luke, and John

[1] These are called "theological" virtues, because, as the great medieval theologian St. Thomas Aquinas once explained, "They have God for their object, both in so far as by them we are properly directed to Him, and because they are infused into our souls by God alone, as also, finally, because we come to know of them only by Divine revelation in the Sacred Scriptures."

Five golden rings	The five books of Moses: Genesis, Exodus, Leviticus, Numbers, Deuteronomy
Six geese-a-laying	God's six days of Creation
Seven swans-a-swimming	Seven gifts of the Holy Spirit
Eight maids-a-milking	Eight Beatitudes[2]
Nine ladies dancing	Nine fruits of the Holy Spirit
Ten lords-a-leaping	The Ten Commandments
Eleven pipers piping	Eleven faithful disciples
Twelve drummers drumming	The twelve sentences, or statements of belief, in the Apostles' Creed

[2] According to Jesus: "Blessed are the poor in spirit, for theirs is the kingdom of heaven. Blessed are those who mourn, for they will be comforted. Blessed are the meek, for they will inherit the land. Blessed are they who hunger and thirst for righteousness, for they will be filled. Blessed are the merciful, for they will receive mercy. Blessed are the pure in heart, for they will see God. Blessed are the peacemakers, for they will be called children of God. Blessed are those who are persecuted for righteousness' sake, for theirs is the kingdom of heaven." (Matthew 5:3–10)

How interesting all of this is! And what a powerful catechism that would be! It wouldn't be such a bad idea to reinvigorate these subtle, coded meanings even today.

"Silent Night, Holy Night" during the twelve days of Christmas might also be a powerful and practical experiment—not in the way that a catechism functions (mostly in the brain, around what we think), but in the way of the heart. "Silent Night" is not coded with hidden meanings, but it quietly instructs us nonetheless, as it sinks into our hearts, and goes to work in our lives.

Each reflection that follows is offered for one of the twelve days of Christmas. Each is meant to accompany the singing—and praying—of one or more of the stanzas of "Silent Night."

CHRISTMAS DAY
Also known as: The Nativity

On this day, like no other day on the calendar during all other times of the year, we are to stop and reflect on the meaning of the Incarnation for our lives. What does Christ's birth in a manger in Bethlehem, on that first silent and holy night, mean in our lives? What does it mean in your life?

Can you envision yourself there, that night? Who might you have been? The innkeeper? Someone whom Joseph and Mary passed along the road?

QUESTIONS TO DISCUSS WITH FRIENDS AND FAMILY

What does Christ's birth in time, more than two thousand years ago, mean for me today? And, Has Christ been born in you? How do you know?

NOW SING ONE OR MORE VERSES OF "SILENT NIGHT."

The Nativity,
vintage engraving

December 26
Also known as: St. Stephen's Day

St. Stephen was the first Christian martyr. The story of his martyrdom in Jerusalem in the year AD 34 is told in the New Testament book of Acts, chapters 6 and 7. His final words were a prayer for his attackers: "Then he knelt down and cried out in a loud voice, 'Lord, do not hold this sin against them.' When he had said this, he died" (Acts 7:60).

In many countries around the world—such as Denmark, Germany, Italy, Macedonia, the Philippines, Poland, Sweden, Ukraine—St. Stephen's Day is still a public holiday.

QUESTIONS TO DISCUSS WITH FRIENDS AND FAMILY
Do you ever feel that your faith puts you at odds with others around you? How? Why?

NOW SING ONE OR MORE VERSES OF "SILENT NIGHT."

December 27

Also known as: The Feast of St. John,
Apostle and Evangelist

In Eastern Orthodox churches, the days between Christmas and Epiphany are supposed to be completely fasting-free. One celebration follows another. For all Christians, these days are a time to celebrate the grace and gifts of God in our lives. Our "silent nights" do not end, but they translate into joy and alleluia.

There is an ancient Epiphany Antiphon from the early church that goes like this:

> Bethlehem born, Nazareth raised,
> He lived in Galilee.
> A sign in the sky, we saw it ourselves.
> How the star shone!
> Shepherds in the fields fell to their knees.
> In amazement, they sang:
> "Glory to the Father, alleluia.
> Glory to the Son and Holy Spirit.
> Alleluia, alleluia, alleluia!"

✳

What are you most thankful for? How does God's presence in your life change who you are, or how you live?

NOW SING ONE OR MORE VERSES OF "SILENT NIGHT."

December 28
Also known as: The Feast of the Holy Innocents

O n this day in history, during the original Christmastide, King Herod ordered the killing of all the male infants in Bethlehem, in a vain attempt to locate the Christ child that he'd heard had been born (see Matthew 2:16–18). As a result, the "Holy Innocents" were murdered that day. Mary, Joseph, and Jesus fled to Egypt.

QUESTIONS TO DISCUSS WITH FRIENDS AND FAMILY

This is a tragic day in history, one that commingles with what's supposed to be a time of great joy. Does your life feel that way, this time of year, combining loss (or memories of loss) with times of happiness and joy? Are you able to talk about that with friends?

NOW SING ONE OR MORE VERSES OF "SILENT NIGHT."

Virgin and Child with the Monkey,
Albrecht Dürer, woodcut, ca. 1498

December 29

Also known as: The Feast of St. Thomas of Canterbury

O
n Easter Sunday, it is common for Christians to greet one another in the following way. Someone might say to you: "Christ is risen." You respond, quickly and confidently: "Christ is risen, indeed!"

A corresponding tradition in Christmastide might be to greet one like this: "Silent night."

You respond, quickly and confidently (but perhaps more quietly than at Easter time), "Silent night, holy night."

QUESTIONS TO DISCUSS WITH FRIENDS AND FAMILY

How is Christmas different from Easter— in your heart, in your experience, in your understanding of your faith?

NOW SING ONE OR MORE VERSES OF "SILENT NIGHT."

December 30
Also known as: The Feast of The Holy Family

Max Lucado writes in his inspirational book *Because of Bethlehem* (2016), "I love Christmas because somewhere someone will ask the Christmas questions: What's the big deal about the baby in the manger?" Then, Lucado tells of his own asking such questions, as a child, and shares beautifully and succinctly the answers he now offers to those who ask: "Because of Bethlehem, I have a Savior in heaven. Christmas begins what Easter celebrates. The child in the cradle became the King on the cross."

QUESTIONS TO DISCUSS WITH FRIENDS AND FAMILY

Consider your own faith, and your own relationship with Christ. Is your faith more of a Christmas sort, or an Easter sort? What is the difference between them; or, is there a difference?

NOW SING ONE OR MORE VERSES OF "SILENT NIGHT."

The Flight into Egypt,
Gustave Doré, engraving, 1891

Holy Family with the Dragonfly,
Albrecht Dürer, woodcut, 1495

Also known as: The Feast of Pope St. Sylvester I

St. Sylvester was the pope who oversaw the First Council of Nicaea, the first ecumenical council in the history of Christianity, and a pivotal moment in the church. From Nicaea (in AD 325) came the Nicene Creed, and our understanding of the relationship between God the Son and God the Father. St. Sylvester was also pope when the emperor Constantine converted to Christianity. Before that happened, it was illegal to be Christian in the Roman Empire, and Christians were publicly executed for witnessing their faith.

Today is a good day to remember those Christians around the world who are unable to worship their Lord in the open, without fear of persecution.

※

Look online for articles about the places in the world today where Christians are being persecuted. You might start with Iran, Iraq, Bhutan, Pakistan, the northern states of Nigeria, and North Korea. What can you do to help them?

NOW SING ONE OR MORE VERSES OF "SILENT NIGHT."

JANUARY 1

Also known as: The Solemnity of Mary, Mother of God

This is a day we celebrate the motherhood of Jesus—Christ's mother, whom many Christians call "Our Lady," the Virgin Mary. She is prominent in the story of the Nativity, and, for that reason, in the opening stanza of "Silent Night." Much of the sense of holy simplicity surrounding the birth of Christ in Bethlehem, and in our odes of praise, come from the personality and spirit of Mary. The Gospel of Luke tells the story simply:

> The angel said to her, "The Holy Spirit will come upon you, and the power of the Most High will overshadow you; therefore the child to be born will be holy; he will be called Son of God." (Luke 1:35)
> Then Mary said, "Here am I, the servant of the Lord; let it be with me according to your word." Then the angel departed from her. (Luke 1:38)

May we all have faith like Mary!

QUESTIONS TO DISCUSS WITH FRIENDS AND FAMILY
Look closely in Luke, chapter 1, when the angel comes to tell Mary what is to happen. Consider Mary's response. What do you make of her response? Was Mary, in some real sense, the first disciple of her Son?

NOW SING ONE OR MORE VERSES OF "SILENT NIGHT."

*Also known as: The Feast of Sts. Basil the Great
and Gregory of Nazianzus*

There are many great hymns for Christmastide. Verse one of "Glory Be to God on High" by John Wesley, first published in London in 1745, goes like this:

> Glory be to God on high,
> > And peace on earth descend;
> God comes down: He bows the sky,
> > And shows Himself our Friend!
> God the invisible appears,
> > God, the blest, the great I AM,
> Sojourns in this vale of tears,
> > And Jesus is His name.

QUESTIONS TO DISCUSS WITH FRIENDS AND FAMILY

What does Jesus bring to earth with his birth in the manger? How is Jesus "the great I AM"? What does it mean that he "Sojourns in this vale of tears"?

NOW SING ONE OR MORE VERSES OF "SILENT NIGHT."

The Holy Family,
Albrecht Dürer, woodcut, 1493–94

January 3

Also known as: The Feast of The Holy Name of Jesus

The fourth and final stanza of that same hymn by John Wesley, goes like this:

We the sons of men rejoice,
  The Prince of Peace proclaim,
With heaven's host lift up our voice,
  And shout *Immanuel's* name:
Knees and hearts to Him we bow,
  Of our flesh, and of our bone,
Jesus is our brother now,
  And God is all our own!

QUESTIONS TO DISCUSS WITH FRIENDS AND FAMILY

How can we proclaim Christ's peace? Do we do that? And what does it mean that "Jesus is our brother now"?

NOW SING ONE OR MORE VERSES OF "SILENT NIGHT."

The German medieval theologian and mystic Meister Eckhart used to say that it is essential for Christians to understand the ultimate purpose of the birth of Christ in the manger—that Christ might be born, not only in Bethlehem, but in us.

QUESTIONS TO DISCUSS WITH FRIENDS AND FAMILY

Is Christ "born" in you? What does that mean for your life? What does that mean *in* your life?

NOW SING ONE OR MORE VERSES OF "SILENT NIGHT."

JANUARY 5

"God has been giving his Son in birth for eternity, in every virtuous soul. God made our souls purposefully to bear his one-begotten Son. When this birth happens now in the good, loving soul of a person, it gives God greater pleasure than His creation of all the heavens and the earth."
—Meister Eckhart

QUESTIONS TO DISCUSS WITH FRIENDS AND FAMILY

What gives God pleasure? How can we live our lives, now, beyond this Christmastide, in ways that give God pleasure?

NOW, BEFORE YOU SING ONE OR MORE VERSES OF "SILENT NIGHT," consider how in the singing you might remain in the spiritual space, place, and spirit of those words, and that music, long after you set down this book. Then, consider keeping on singing these words.

In *Bread in the Wilderness,* Thomas Merton wrote that, as a monk, the Book of Psalms had a greater hold on his life ("an accidental advantage," he called it) than did the words of the New Testament, because Psalms were words that monks sing, not just read.

The Magi,
Gustave Doré, engraving, 1891

The Adoration of the Wise Man,
Albrecht Dürer, woodcut, 1524

MORE READING

ON THE HISTORY OF CHRISTMAS CAROLS:

The Carols of Christmas: A Celebration of the Surprising Stories Behind Your Favorite Holiday Songs

By Andrew Gant (Thomas Nelson, 2015)

By an Oxford professor and renowned English musician, this book appeals to those with a serious interest in Christmas carols. Fellow musicians won't be disappointed, either, as there are occasional technical details. Does not include a chapter on "Silent Night," however!

ON THE ART OF THE NATIVITY:

Art of the Crèche: Nativities from Around the World
By James L. Govan (Merrell, 2009)

Worth seeing and reading, and not just for those who collect Nativity creches. Includes examples from all over the world, including Russia, New Zealand, and Peru, each with local and interesting details. Photographs throughout.

Wounded in Spirit: Advent Art and Meditations
By David Bannon (Paraclete Press, 2018)

Written and designed for those who relive moments of loss at Christmas. Based on the latest research in history and grief, *Wounded in Spirit* returns you to where Christian art began. From mourning in Roman catacombs to works of the masters, you join the world's great religious artists on their pilgrimages of hope and brokenness, to again encounter "God with us."

ON BETHLEHEM, THE BIRTH OF JESUS, CAESAR AUGUSTUS, ETC.:

The First Days of Jesus: The Story of the Incarnation
By Andreas J. Köstenberger and Alexander Stewart (Crossway, 2015)

A well-written book, but intended only for those seeking to undertake serious study of the original setting, era, historical figures, and the theological implications of the birth of Christ in Bethlehem.

ON "SILENT NIGHT, HOLY NIGHT":

Silent Night: The Song and Its Story
By Margaret Hodges, Illustrated by Tim Ladwig
(Eerdmans, 2001)

This beautiful children's book offers the best
overview of how the Christmas carol came to be.
It is now, sadly, out of print, but go find a copy and
read it, not only with children, but with adults as
well.

The Holy Family in a Stable,
Albrecht Dürer, woodcut, 1504

As we mentioned at the outset, no Christmas carol has been recorded more often than "Silent Night, Holy Night." There are many, many exemplary recordings you can listen to. At the end of chapter 1, we shared with you the first of them, by the great Haydn Quartet, from 1905. All of these, too, we know, are wonderful. Listen to them if you can.

Kathleen Battle (soprano) and *Christopher Parkening* (guitar)
First released on the album *Angels' Glory: Christmas Music for Voice and Guitar*.
1996

Al Green (singing)
First released on *The Christmas Album*.
1983

The Temptations (singing)
First released on the album *Give Love at Christmas*.
It was the final track.
1980

Mormon Tabernacle Choir (singing)
From *Silent Night: The Greatest Hits of Christmas*
1980

Gloriæ Dei Cantores (choir and organ)
From *Keeping Christmas: Beloved Carols and the Christmas Story*. This arrangement for organ is a highlight in a collection of carols sung by the choir and enhanced by traditional Scripture readings for Christmas.
2010

MORE WORSHIPING

Every urban or rural, city or country, parish or circuit or house church is beautiful during Christmastide. There is nothing lovelier than worshiping with others—friends, family, and strangers—who share our passion for Jesus Christ. If you have the opportunity someday to visit one of these cathedrals, abbeys, and otherwise famous churches around the world, do so—and not simply to see the art and appreciate the architecture, but for worship. Singing "Silent Night" with brothers and sisters in Christ at each of these places is a special experience every year.

Westminster Cathedral, London, England
(Church of England)
www.westminstercathedral.org.uk

Saint Patrick's Cathedral, Dublin, Ireland
(Roman Catholic)
www.stpatrickscathedral.ie

Buckfast Abbey, near Devon, England
(Roman Catholic)
www.buckfast.org.uk

St. Peter's Basilica, Vatican City
(Roman Catholic)
www.vatican.va/various/basiliche/san_pietro/
index_it.htm

Notre-Dame Basilica, Montreal, Canada
(Roman Catholic)
www.basiliquenotredame.ca/en

Church of Mary Magdalene, Jerusalem
(Russian Orthodox)
www.russgefsimania.com/mobile.html

Storkyrkan (The Church of Saint Nicholas),
Stockholm, Sweden (Church of Sweden)

La Sagrada Família, Barcelona, Spain
(Roman Catholic)
www.sagradafamilia.org

The Church of the Transfiguration, Orleans,
Massachusetts, USA (Benedictine ecumenical)
Gloriæ Dei Cantores sings the traditional service
of Advent Lessons and Carols here every year.
www.churchofthetransfiguration.org
www.gdcchoir.org

St. Patrick's Cathedral, New York, New York, USA (Roman Catholic)
www.saintpatrickscathedral.org

St. Thomas Church, New York, New York, USA (Episcopalian)
www.saintthomaschurch.org

Fourth Presbyterian Church, Chicago, Illinois, USA (Presbyterian)
www.fourthchurch.org

The Metropolitan Cathedral of Saint Sebastian, Rio de Janiero, Brazil (Roman Catholic)
www.catedral.com.br

ABOUT PARACLETE PRESS

WHO WE ARE

As the publishing arm of the Community of Jesus, Paraclete Press presents a full expression of Christian belief and practice—from Catholic to Evangelical, from Protestant to Orthodox, reflecting the ecumenical charism of the Community and its dedication to sacred music, the fine arts, and the written word. We publish books, recordings, sheet music, and video/DVDs that nourish the vibrant life of the church and its people.

WHAT WE ARE DOING
Books

PARACLETE PRESS BOOKS show the richness and depth of what it means to be Christian. While Benedictine spirituality is at the heart of who we are and all that we do, our books reflect the Christian experience across many cultures, time periods, and houses of worship.

We have many series, including *Paraclete Essentials; Paraclete Fiction; Paraclete Poetry; Paraclete Giants;* and for children and adults, *All God's Creatures,* books about animals and faith; and *San Damiano Books,* focusing on Franciscan spirituality. Others include *Voices from the Monastery* (men and women monastics writing about living a spiritual life today), *Active Prayer,* and new for young readers: *The Pope's Cat.* We also specialize in gift books for children on the occasions of Baptism and First Communion, as well as other important times in a child's life, and books that bring creativity and liveliness to any adult spiritual life.

The Mount Tabor Books series focuses on the arts and literature as well as liturgical worship and spirituality; it was created in conjunction with the Mount Tabor Ecumenical Centre for Art and Spirituality in Barga, Italy.

Music

THE PARACLETE RECORDINGS label represents the internationally acclaimed choir *Gloriæ Dei Cantores*, the *Gloriæ Dei Cantores Schola*, and the other instrumental artists of the *Arts Empowering Life Foundation*.

Paraclete Press is the exclusive North American distributor for the Gregorian chant recordings from St. Peter's Abbey in Solesmes, France. Paraclete also carries all of the Solesmes chant publications for Mass and the Divine Office, as well as their academic research publications.

In addition, PARACLETE PRESS SHEET MUSIC publishes the work of today's finest composers of sacred choral music, annually reviewing over 1,000 works and releasing between 40 and 60 works for both choir and organ.

Video

Our video/DVDs offer spiritual help, healing, and biblical guidance for a broad range of life issues including grief and loss, marriage, forgiveness, facing death, understanding suicide, bullying, addictions, Alzheimer's, and Christian formation.

Learn more about us at our website:
www.paracletepress.com,
or call us toll-free at 1-800-451-5006.

SCAN
TO
READ
MORE